"A Life Worth Living Series"

Taking Out The Garbage
Leaving Your Past

Ross Brodfuehrer

Lessons are numbered Week 11 to Week 17, consistent with use as a
sequel to *Charting Your Course*, but this book may be used by itself,
even if you have not gone through the earlier book.

International Standard Book Number (ISBN): 0-89900-837-2

T rash.
 A basic commodity of all life.
 No town is free of it.
 No home without it.
 No life untouched by it.

The broken pickle jar.   The empty milk carton.
The black banana peel.   The sloggy coffee grounds.
 The overfull diaper.   The clumpy cat litter.
 The fuzzy green, unidentifiable leftovers
  found in the back of the refrigerator.

No one wants this stuff.
Not even the poorest of homeless garbage pickers.
 Yet some keep the stinking stuff.
  Even stockpile it.
And not even at the back property line,
  in their own landfill.
 No, right in the living room of their hearts.

Taking out the garbage is a basic task of every teenager's life.
Yet many adults have left the chore undone.
And so their lives are junked up.
 Embarrassingly unsanitary inside.
  And beginning to draw flies.

But just as we tell our kids —
 It is never too late to haul out the garbage.

That is especially true when our Chief Garbage Collector works seven
days a week. He never refuses our refuse.
 Not matter how high the mountain of moldy muck,
  it is never higher than Golgotha.
Every day is trash day with him.

Acknowledgments

Thanks to my parents, Ervin and Nancy Brodfuehrer, who made me carry out the garbage regularly, chew soap occasionally (after a foul word or two) and, most importantly, go to church weekly, where I learned how much I had to dump, and just how to do it.

Further thanks to Rich, Greg, Joe and Eugene who haven't hesitated to point out my garbage (always with great gentleness, of course) and still continued to hold onto our friendship even while holding their noses. I hereby nominate you all for "Associate Garbage Men of the Decade" Awards. The 'Golden Trash Can' will look great on your desks.

FACING THE PAST

Get Real with Your Past

A large, invisible backpack rests on the shoulders of most people. The backpack itself is not seen, but its cumbersome, tiring effects are quite evident.

The pack is our past memories, failures, guilt feelings, sins, scars, broken dreams, lost hopes. We carry these memories like a ball and chain, and seem unable to find the key to unlock the burden and walk free.

In the pack are heavy rocks we use to stone ourselves over and over for the failures we have had. Also in the bag are videos of scenes of past failures and cassette tapes of condemning voices saying, "You will never get it right. Why can't you ever learn? You're no good." It seems we only watch the bad reruns.

That's no way for a Christian to live. Christ never intended us to be shackled to the past. It is Satan the accuser who likes to rub our noses in the dirt. God wants to lift our eyes to the heavens.

Jesus changed the names of his followers so they would know that they could leave their pasts in the past. Second Corinthians 5:17 says, "If anyone is in Christ, he is a new creation; the old has gone, the new has come!" The Lord said that we are not to "pour new wine into old wineskins." (Matthew 9:17) Paul said, "Forgetting what is behind and straining toward what is ahead, I press on toward the goal to win the prize for which God has called me heavenward in Christ Jesus." (Philippians 3:13)

The past is like a goblin: it has no power to hurt us unless we believe in it and give it power. But God's love drives out fear and gives us a future. Release your past this week!

MONDAY

FOCUS:
Father, I praise you for being the Lord of my past as well as my present and future.

We have a God who loves to change people's pitiful pasts into potent presents. Let's begin our week by looking at Paul and his ugly past.

How would you describe Paul (originally called Saul) from Acts 7:55–8:3 and 9:1-2?

"⁵⁵But Stephen, full of the Holy Spirit, looked up to heaven and saw the glory of God, and Jesus standing at the right hand of God. ⁵⁶'Look,' he said, 'I see heaven open and the Son of Man standing at the right hand of God.'

"⁵⁷At this they covered their ears and, yelling at the top of their voices, they all rushed at him, ⁵⁸dragged him out of the city and began to stone him. Meanwhile, the witnesses laid their clothes at the feet of a young man named Saul.

"⁵⁹While they were stoning him, Stephen prayed, 'Lord Jesus, receive my spirit.' ⁶⁰Then he fell on his knees and cried out, 'Lord, do not hold this sin against them.' When he had said this, he fell asleep. ¹And Saul was there, giving approval to his death.

"On that day a great persecution broke out against the church at Jerusalem, and all except the apostles were scattered throughout Judea and Samaria. ²Godly men buried Stephen and mourned deeply for him. ³But Saul began to destroy the church. Going from house to house, he dragged off men and women and put them in prison."

"¹Meanwhile, Saul was still breathing out murderous threats against the Lord's disciples. He went to the high priest ²and asked him for letters to the synagogues in Damascus, so that if he found any there who belonged to the Way, whether men or women, he might take them as prisoners to Jerusalem."

Whom do you know today who you would say is like Saul?

Contrast man's reaction to a person like Saul with God's concern for him in Acts 9:3-19.

"³As he neared Damascus on his journey, suddenly a light from heaven flashed around him. ⁴He fell to the ground and heard a voice say to him, 'Saul, Saul, why do you persecute me?'

"⁵'Who are you, Lord?' Saul asked.

"'I am Jesus, whom you are persecuting,' he replied. ⁶'Now get up and go into the city, and you will be told what you must do.'

"⁷The men traveling with Saul stood there speechless; they heard the sound but did not see anyone. ⁸Saul got up from the ground, but when he opened his eyes he could see nothing. So they led him by the hand into Damascus. ⁹For three days he was blind, and did not eat or drink anything.

"¹⁰In Damascus there was a disciple named Ananias. The Lord called to him in a vision, 'Ananias!'

"'Yes, Lord,' he answered.

"¹¹The Lord told him, 'Go to the house of Judas on Straight Street and ask for a man from Tarsus named Saul, for he is praying. ¹²In a vision he has seen a man named Ananias come and place his hands on him to restore his sight.'

"¹³'Lord,' Ananias answered, 'I have heard many reports about this man and all the harm he has done to your saints in Jerusalem. ¹⁴And he has come here with authority from the chief priests to arrest all who call on your name.'

"¹⁵But the Lord said to Ananais, 'Go! This man is my chosen instrument to carry my name before the Gentiles and their kings and before the people of Israel. ¹⁶I will show him how much he must suffer for my name.'

"¹⁷Then Ananias went to the house and entered it. Placing his hands on Saul, he said, 'Brother Saul, the Lord — Jesus, who appeared to you on the road as you were coming here — has sent me so that you may see again and be filled with the Holy Spirit. ¹⁸Immediately, something like scales fell from Saul's eyes, and he could see again. He got up and was baptized, and after taking some food, he regained his strength."

To what extent did Jesus go to reach Saul and give him a new start? What was Ananias' reaction to meeting Saul?

JESUS	ANANIAS

Do people hold your past against you? Think through these people, and decide whether they generally believe you will be as you have always been or they believe you can and are being transformed like Saul.

Your mother _____

Your father _____

Your spouse _____

Your children _____

Your friends _____

Yourself _____

But God is not like man. Jesus wanted Saul to be changed. He knew it could be done, and it was done. What is God's belief about you — that you will always be the same or that you will be different?

_____

PRAYER:
Father, whom will I believe — people or you? Whose estimation of me will I accept — the human or the divine?

10

TUESDAY

FOCUS:
Thank you for being a forgiving and forgetting God.

Line your past up against Saul's today. Thoughtfully list your worst failures, sins and mistakes of the past beside Saul's.

SAUL   MINE

1. self-righteous

2. egotistical

3. mean

4. blasphemer

5. violent

6. persecutor of the church

7. arrested women and children

8. murderer

Why does Paul say he was shown mercy in 1 Timothy 1:12-17, especially verse 16?

"¹²I thank Christ Jesus our Lord, who has given me strength, that he considered me faithful, appointing me to his service. ¹³Even though I was once a blasphemer and a persecutor and a violent man, I was shown mercy because I acted in ignorance and unbelief. ¹⁴The grace of our Lord was poured out on me abundantly, along with the faith and love that are in Christ Jesus.

"¹⁵Here is a trustworthy saying that deserves full acceptance: Christ Jesus came into the world to save sinners — of whom I am the worst. ¹⁶But for that reason I was shown mercy so that in me, the worst of sinners, Christ Jesus might display his unlimited patience as an example for those who would believe on him and receive eternal life. ¹⁷Now to the King eternal, immortal, invisible, the only God, be honor and glory for ever and ever. Amen."

If you do not allow God to erase your past, then are you saying . . .

    a) Your past is worse than Saul's.

    b) God has changed and no longer forgets people's pasts.

    c) You can't let your past go due to your own guilt.

    d) You don't deserve it.

Many times it is difficult for us to let go of the past because we keep on repeating it. We continue to do the same old, dumb things we did 10 or even 20 years ago. But God's forgiveness is not based upon our ongoing performance. If it were, then our past would only be forgiven if we became near perfect in the present. What are your chances of becoming perfect? If you were a Las Vegas oddsmaker, what odds would you give yourself? _____

PRAYER:
Lord, help me to trust your grace rather than my works.

FOCUS:
Release yesterday to God and his grace.

A child discovers that the best way to make mom happy is to color in the lines or be seen but not heard. That pattern for pleasing people continues throughout life. Or a child finds that he gets attention by clowning or causing a ruckus. He continues getting attention this way into adulthood.

In effect, we "signed" these important belief contracts when we were limited in knowledge and experience. We were incompetent. Yet we keep living out the stipulations of the contracts year after year.

What does Paul tell us in 1 Corinthians 13:11?
"When I was a child, I talked like a child, I thought like a child, I reasoned like a child. When I became a man, I put childish ways behind me."

_____

_____

_____

What contracts did you sign in childhood? Do you still live them? Test yourself by choosing two or three areas from the following list, writing what you came to believe about them as a child, then determining if you still believe and live that way.

- The importance of money

- Your view of lazy people

- How to handle conflict

- The value of a good education

- What you think of poor people

- Your own worth and potential

- What God is like

My Contracts

_____
_____
_____
_____
_____
_____
_____
_____
_____
_____
_____
_____
_____
_____
_____
_____
_____
_____
_____
_____
_____
_____
_____
_____
_____

Prayerfully read 1 Corinthians 13 and "sign it" as your new contract of how you will live.

_____

THURSDAY

FOCUS:
Even yesterday is now the past. I can't relive it or revise it. But I don't have to repeat it.

Some people are not able to release the past because they never fully faced and confessed the guilt of their sin. Others can't release it because they have never fully forgiven others of their offenses against them.

Today we will attempt to find and confess any unresolved guilt in our own lives. Tomorrow we focus on forgiving people from our pasts.

Summarize the truths you find in Psalm 32 in the space below
"¹Blessed is he whose transgressions are forgiven, whose sins are covered. ²Blessed is the man whose sin the LORD does not count against him and in whose spirit is no deceit.

"³When I kept silent, my bones wasted away through my groaning all day long. ⁴For day and night your hand was heavy upon me; my strength was sapped as in the heat of summer. ⁵Then I acknowledged my sin to you and did not cover up my iniquity. I said, 'I will confess my transgressions to the LORD' — and you forgave the guilt of my sin.

"⁶Therefore, let everyone who is godly pray to you while you may be found; surely when the mighty waters rise, they will not reach him. ⁷You are my hiding place; you will protect me from trouble and surround me with songs of deliverance.

"⁸I will instruct you and teach you in the way you should go; I will counsel you and watch over you. ⁹Do not be like the horse or the mule, which have no understanding but must be controlled by bit and bridle or they will not come to you. ¹⁰Many are the woes of the wicked, but the LORD's unfailing love surrounds the man who trusts in him. ¹¹Rejoice in the LORD, and be glad, you righteous; sing, all you who are upright in heart!"

_____
_____
_____
_____
_____

Do verses 3-4 describe any area of your life? Do you feel guilt, weakness, weight in any of the following areas:

___ relationally: Is there anyone you have hurt, cheated, used, let down, and have not reconciled it?

___ sexually: Is there promiscuity in your past that you still carry with you — premarital sex, using others for your pleasure, pornography?

___ financially: Have you used money selfishly, loved it too much, lied to get it in your past?

___ spiritually: Do you feel you have let God down, fallen short of his plan for your life, smeared his name with some of your actions?

PRAYER:
Ask God for insight right now to mentally walk through your life, beginning with your earliest memories. Ask God to point out to you any sin on your part for which you have not confessed openly to him and received forgiveness.

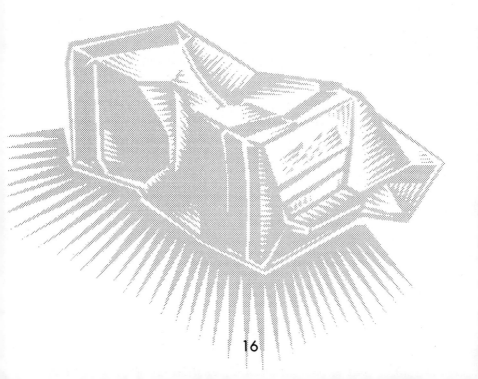

FRIDAY

FOCUS:
If you did yesterday's assignment, then you can thank God right now that you are fully clean, free, forgiven and whiter than snow!

What message does God give you in Matthew 18:21-35?

Dear _____ :

Sincerely,

God

"²¹Then Peter came to Jesus and asked, 'Lord, how many times shall I forgive my brother when he sins against me? Up to seven times?'

"²²Jesus answered, 'I tell you, not seven times, but seventy-seven times.

"²³Therefore, the kingdom of heaven is like a king who wanted to settle accounts with his servants. ²⁴As he began the settlement, a man who owed him ten thousand talents was brought to him. ²⁵Since he was not able to pay, the master ordered that he and his wife and his children and all that he had be sold to repay the debt.

"²⁶The servant fell on his knees before him. 'Be patient with me,' he begged, 'and I will pay back everything.' ²⁷The servant's master took pity on him, canceled the debt and let him go.

"²⁸But when that servant went out, he found one of his fellow servants who owed him a hundred denarii. He grabbed him and began to choke him. 'Pay back what you owe me!' he demanded.

"²⁹His fellow servant fell to his knees and begged him, 'Be patient with me, and I will pay you back.'

"³⁰But he refused. Instead, he went off and had the man thrown into prison until he could pay the debt. ³¹When the other servants saw what had happened, they were greatly distressed and went and told their master everything that had happened.

"³²Then the master called the servant in. 'You wicked servant,' he said, 'I canceled all that debt of yours because you begged me to. ³³Shouldn't you have had mercy on your fellow servant just as I had on you?' ³⁴In anger his master turned him over to the jailers to be tortured, until he should pay back all he owed.

"³⁵This is how my heavenly Father will treat each of you unless you forgive your brother from your heart.'"

Write the names of the ten most significant people in your past. As you write each name, give yourself an honest "gut check." What does your spirit feel toward that person? If it is totally positive, put a "+" in the space after the name. If it is very negative, put a "−" in the space. If you feel a mixture, put "+/−."

1. _____   _____

2. _____   _____

3. _____   _____

4. _____   _____

5. _____   _____

6. _____   _____

7. _____   _____

8. _____   _____

9. _____   _____

10. _____   _____

PRAYER:

For those names where you placed a negative symbol, consider if there is anything for which you have not forgiven them. Forgiveness does not mean that you forget; it does mean that you release your grudge and will treat them with the same attitude God treats you. Forgiving the people in your past may be the key to moving on to a new and free future.

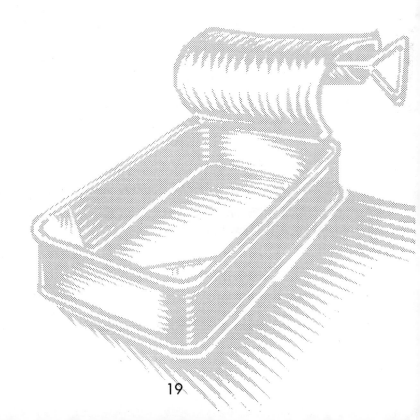

TAKING OUT THE GARBAGE

Releasing the Past

D o you need to release something, anything, from your past? Maybe you are one of the millions mangled by the massive accident called "modern society." Maybe you're a firsthand casualty of workaholic parents. Maybe you've been amputated just above the heart in a custody battle. Maybe you've been blindsided by a substance-abusing dad or simply left for dead by a swinging single mom.

Or maybe you came from one of the increasingly shrinking number of "healthy" homes, with a dad who would rather be head of the home than head of the home office, and a mom who would rather hang around the family room raising her kids than around the barroom raising Cain.

Either way, no past is perfect. Even with the best of pasts, if we don't understand them, we will be doomed to repeat them — the good, the bad and the ugly. Learn to live today for all it can be by seeing yesterday for all it was. If you don't, the past can become:

- a box: whatever has been is all that can be.

- a nightmare that you relive in your daydreams today.

- a ball and chain, with the extra weight of guilt, habit, or anger slowing you down and wearing you out.

- an upset bone, once broken, now healed, but crooked.

- an empty cup of needs never really fulfilled.

- an instant replay with the present simply the past regurgitated.

Tomorrow can be different. "If anyone is in Christ, he is a new creation; the old has gone, the new has come!"

MONDAY

FOCUS:
What's been most on your mind lately? Talk it over with Jesus.

The Bible tells it like it is. No candy coating the characters. No air brushing the true historical picture. No Bible-gate cover-ups. No Hollywood romanticizing. Just the facts, ma'am.

Speed read Genesis 27 through 35:15. If you have not read it before, you will most likely find it interesting, intriguing, even fascinating, not to mention shocking, saddening and soap opera-esque at times. If you have read it before, think of how you would feel about the story if it were describing your immediate family!

Write down a few of the "real history" types of things about your family, the stuff no glossy PR person would write.

_____

_____

_____

The only way to release the past is to first GET REAL WITH THE PAST. Nobody has a perfect past. So stop fairytale-izing your past. Tell yourself the truth about it. For example, children first see their parents as heroes who can do no wrong; as adolescents, they see parents as Neros who just want to dictate; and then in their early 20s, as zeros who have nothing worthwhile to contribute to their lives. But they may never come to see their parents for what they are, simply as humans, who did some good things and some bad things.

PRAYER:
Honestly, before God, describe:

Your mom:_____

_____

21

Your dad: _____

_____

Your childhood: _____

_____

_____

Your family atmosphere:_____

_____

_____

Your family rules:_____

_____

TUESDAY

FOCUS:
Ask God to show you what "speaking the truth in love" (Ephesians 4:15) means for someone trying to release the past.

Today, skim chapter 37 in Genesis, highlighting what happens to Joseph as a result of his brothers' betrayal.

_____

_____

_____

Genesis 42:21 describes a bit of Joseph's personal reaction to his abduction.

"They said to one another, 'Surely we are being punished because of our brother. We saw how distressed he was when he pleaded with us for his life, but we would not listen; that's why this distress has come upon us.'"

What do you imagine were some of his thoughts, feelings and fears during his ordeal?

_____

_____

_____

Because of his brothers' cruelty, Joseph not only becomes slave labor, but ends up in prison for several years as well! As a matter of fact, 13 of Joseph's best years, from age 17 to 30, when he should have been at home with family and friends, are lost in the foreign legion of Egypt's slavery. Until, by God's providence, Joseph is raised to be Pharaoh's second in command. Then his brothers show up in Egypt to buy his grain! Does Joseph forgive right away? Read what he does in Genesis 42–44 (more speed reading!) and try to think of why he does all this.

TO FORGIVE IS NOT THE SAME AS SAYING, "I'LL JUST FORGET IT BECAUSE . . .

____ it's no big deal."

____ it was probably all my fault."

____ they didn't mean to hurt me."

____ others have endured worse."

____ they are my family."

____ it hurts too badly to remember."

____ they did their best."

 PRAYER:
How have you dealt with your past hurts?

WEDNESDAY

FOCUS:
Finish this sentence, "Heavenly Father, I love you because . . ."

"Honor your father and your mother," the Bible says. How do you honor them while at the same time, honestly assessing where they hurt you in the past? A key is in understanding that "honoring" is not the same as ignoring what has happened or pretending everything is hunky-dory. To pretend our parents, grandparents, or siblings were perfect is not honoring to them; it is just plain self-deception. True honoring comes when we see people for who they truly were and are, warts and all, then choose to deal with them kindly yet honestly, considerately yet straightforwardly.

How would you apply each of these Scriptures in dealing with people who have hurt you in the past?

Proverbs 27:6 _____

_____

1 Timothy 5:1 _____

_____

Matthew 18:15-16 _____

_____

We will never be free from our past until we face our past. To face it, we must stop protecting our parents and families, and see them as they really were. Some people feel they would break family loyalty to think their parents wrong, sinful, or weak. They don't want to betray their parents, but are betraying truth to defend their parents.

To best honor your folks, you must forgive your folks. But you cannot forgive what you do not first feel. TO FORGIVE IT, YOU MUST FIRST FACE IT, THEN FEEL IT.

PRAYER:
Ask God how he feels about your past pains, how he sees your childhood upbringing, the way he views your family of origin.

THURSDAY

FOCUS:
Use the "Lord's Prayer" as your guide (Matthew 6:9-13).

Who best represents you in the parable of Matthew 18:21-35?

"²¹Then Peter came to Jesus and asked, 'Lord, how many times shall I forgive my brother when he sins against me? Up to seven times?'

"²²Jesus answered, 'I tell you, not seven times, but seventy-seven times.

"²³Therefore, the kingdom of heaven is like a king who wanted to settle accounts with his servants. ²⁴As he began the settlement, a man who owed him ten thousand talents was brought to him. ²⁵Since he was not able to pay, the master ordered that he and his wife and his children and all that he had be sold to repay the debt.

"²⁶The servant fell on his knees before him. 'Be patient with me,' he begged, 'and I will pay back everything.' ²⁷The servant's master took pity on him, canceled the debt and let him go.

"²⁸But when that servant went out, he found one of his fellow servants who owed him a hundred denarii. He grabbed him and began to choke him. 'Pay back what you owe me!' he demanded.

"²⁹His fellow servant fell to his knees and begged him, 'Be patient with me, and I will pay you back.'

"³⁰But he refused. Instead, he went off and had the man thrown into prison until he could pay the debt. ³¹When the other servants saw what had happened, they were greatly distressed and went and told their master everything that had happened.

"³²Then the master called the servant in. 'You wicked servant,' he said, 'I canceled all that debt of yours because you begged me to. ³³Shouldn't you have had mercy on your fellow servant just as I had on you?' ³⁴In anger his master turned him over to the jailers to be tortured, until he should pay back all he owed.

"³⁵This is how my heavenly Father will treat each of you unless you forgive your brother from your heart.'"

Name the person: _____

List the "debts" you have owed to God in your life, the sins you have sinned all along the way, your mistakes, failures, offenses against others, etc. Write in as many as you can fit in the space below.

If you did not fill up the space, ask God to show you anything else in you that has displeased him in the past or the present.

Circle the sins, mistakes, failures that you truly want God to forgive.

Is there anything for which you have not forgiven someone? List it here.

PRAYER:
Act on Matthew 18:21-22 and 35.

FRIDAY

FOCUS:
Father, show me the freedom I can have when I truly assess the hurts done against me, feel them, and decisively forgive from the heart.

List five of the worst hurts that have ever been done to you.

1. _____

2. _____

3. _____

4. _____

5. _____

Read Romans 8:28. ("And we know that in all things God works for the good of those who love him, who have been called according to his purpose.") Do you believe it?

_____ Yes   _____ No

What good did God bring out of Joseph's trials (Genesis 47)?

_____

_____

_____

Can you imagine saying and doing to those who hurt you the same things that Joseph says and does to his brothers:

_____ Come close to me (verse 4).

_____ Do not be angry with yourselves (verse 5).

_____ I will provide for you (verse 11).

_____ Kissed them (verse 15).

28

You can only say and do these things if you can say also what he says in 50:19-20.

"But Joseph said to them, 'Don't be afraid. Am I in the place of God? You intended to harm me, but God intended it for good to accomplish what is now being done, the saving of many lives.'"

Can you see something good God has brought in each of the five terrible things you listed above?

1. _____

2. _____

3. _____

4. _____

5. _____

 PRAYER:
Express your belief in God's promises and thank him for turning your pain into his power.

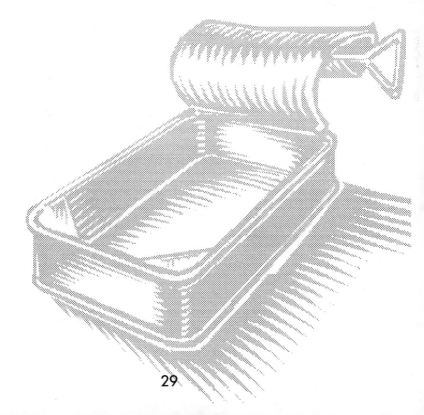

GIVE IT UP!

The Road to Recovery

Our message this week flies in the face of modern culture. Schools teach that we have unlimited potential. Motivational speakers earn big bucks traveling the country with their message of personal power. New Age gurus instruct us that we have this spark of God inside, and we can create our own reality.

Admitting we are powerless is certainly anti-American (unless you want to call yourself a "victim" in order to receive special treatment). We love power. Superheroes are always a national favorite. Popular video games give kids the feeling of power by fighting, shooting and mutilating their on-screen opponents. Concealed weapons bills have become law in some states, giving citizens the power to protect themselves.

Even Christian leaders and church members get caught up in the "you can do it if you only try and believe in yourself" mentality. We parrot the old line, "God helps those who help themselves," not realizing that the Bible never says that. A more scriptural truth is, "God helps those who admit they can't help themselves."

Is that a difficult idea for you to accept? Does it cut against your do-it-yourself grain?

Just what are we powerless to do? We can certainly breathe, eat, work, build a house or business or increase our physical endurance. There are lots of things we can do. How are we powerless?

Find out this week in our study (unless you are powerless to discipline yourself to do it).

MONDAY

FOCUS:
"Not the labor of my hands can fulfill Thy law's demands. Could my zeal no respite know; could my tears forever flow; all for sin could not atone. Thou must save and Thou alone."

Powerless to Live Holy Lives

Write a synopsis of Paul's words in Romans 7:14-25.

"[14]We know that the law is spiritual; but I am unspiritual, sold as a slave to sin. [15]I do not understand what I do. For what I want to do I do not do, but what I hate I do. [16]And if I do what I do not want to do, I agree that the law is good. [17]As it is, it is no longer I myself who do it, but it is sin living in me. [18]I know that nothing good lives in me, that is, in my sinful nature. For I have the desire to do what is good, but I cannot carry it out. [19]For what I do is not the good I want to do; no, the evil I do not want to do — this I keep on doing. [20]Now if I do what I do not want to do, it is no longer I who do it, but it is sin living in me that does it.

"[21]So I find this law at work: When I want to do good, evil is right there with me. [22]For in my inner being I delight in God's law; [23]but I see another law at work in the members of my body, waging war against the law of my mind and making me a prisoner of the law of sin at work within my members. [24]What a wretched man I am! Who will rescue me from this body of death? [25]Thanks be to God — through Jesus Christ our Lord!

"So then, I myself in my mind am a slave to God's law, but in the sinful nature a slave to the law of sin."

If you could sign this "confession" too, do so.

_____

We will never put our trust in Christ until we have despaired of ourselves. Have you despaired of your powerlessness to be holy?

❑ Yes   ❑ No   ❑ Sort of

In the passage you just read, the emphasis was on "I" and "me." Note quickly how many times the personal pronoun is used. But in the next chapter, 8:5-17, who is the emphasis on, and what does he do?

"⁵Those who live according to the sinful nature have their minds set on what that nature desires; but those who live in accordance with the Spirit have their minds set on what the Spirit desires. ⁶The mind of sinful man is death, but the mind controlled by the Spirit is life and peace; ⁷the sinful mind is hostile to God. It does not submit to God's law, nor can it do so. ⁸Those controlled by the sinful nature cannot please God.

"⁹You, however, are controlled not by the sinful nature but by the Spirit, if the Spirit of God lives in you. And if anyone does not have the Spirit of Christ, he does not belong to Christ. ¹⁰But if Christ is in you, your body is dead because of sin, yet your spirit is alive because of righteousness. ¹¹And if the Spirit of him who raised Jesus from the dead is living in you, he who raised Christ from the dead will also give life to your mortal bodies through his spirit, who lives in you.

"¹²Therefore, brothers, we have an obligation — but it is not to the sinful nature, to live according to it. ¹³For if you live according to the sinful nature, you will die; but if by the Spirit you put to death the misdeeds of the body, you will live, ¹⁴because those who are led by the Spirit of God are sons of God. ¹⁵For you did not receive a spirit that makes you a slave again to fear, but you received the Spirit of sonship. And by him we cry, 'Abba, Father.' ¹⁶The Spirit himself testifies with our spirit that we are God's children. ¹⁷Now if we are children, then we are heirs — heirs of God and co-heirs with Christ, if indeed we share in his sufferings in order that we may also share in his glory."

_____

_____

_____

How much would you say you lean on and utilize the Holy Spirit's power in your life? Shade in the scale below to the proper level.

10%	20%	30%	40%	50%	60%	70%	80%	90%	100%

Is God pleased with the level of your reliance on him?

 PRAYER:
What will you do about it?

TUESDAY

FOCUS:
"Nothing in my hand I bring; simply to Thy cross I cling. Naked, come to Thee for dress; helpless look to Thee for grace; foul, I to the fountain fly. Wash me, Savior, or I die!"

Powerless to Love God with All Our Heart, Soul, Mind and Strength

In Mark 12:28-34, how important is the greatest commandment?

"^{28}One of the teachers of the law came and heard them debating. Noticing that Jesus had given them a good answer, he asked him, 'Of all the commandments, which is the most important?'

"^{29}'The most important one,' answered Jesus, 'is this: "Hear, O Israel, the Lord our God, the Lord is one. ^{30}Love the Lord your God with all your heart and with all your soul and with all your mind and with all your strength." ^{31}The second is this: "Love your neighbor as yourself." There is no commandment greater than these.'

"^{32}'Well said, teacher,' the man replied. 'You are right in saying that God is one and there is no other but him. ^{33}To love him with all your heart, with all your understanding and with all your strength, and to love your neighbor as yourself is more important than all burnt offerings and sacrifices.'

"^{34}When Jesus saw that he had answered wisely, he said to him, 'You are not far from the kingdom of God.' And from then on no one dared ask him any more questions."

What does Jesus say about this command in Matthew 22:40? ("All the Law and the Prophets hang on these two commandments.")

When you wake up every morning, what do you think about first? What do you focus on? On most days, what are your goals? Put one word in the center of the target.

Which of the following is most on your mind each day? Number 1 to 5.

___ self ___ work ___ family

___ others ___ God

Do you feel like a failure because you just can't keep God first in your life, your focus continually slips away to other things, even while praying or attending church?

 We fail because of the truth we studied yesterday. Admit to God that you cannot love him. Ask him for the power of the Holy Spirit to do what you cannot do on your own. Expect to receive this power today.

WEDNESDAY

FOCUS:
"Rock of Ages, cleft for me, let me hide myself in Thee. Let the water and the blood, from Thy wounded side which flowed, be of sin the double cure, cleanse me from its guilt and power."

Powerless to Love Our Neighbors as Ourselves

Who is the neighbor in Luke 10:25-37?

"²⁵On one occasion an expert in the law stood up to test Jesus. 'Teacher,' he asked, 'what must I do to inherit eternal life?'

"²⁶'What is written in the Law?' He replied. 'How do you read it?' ²⁷He answered: '"Love the Lord your God with all your heart and with all your soul and with all your strength and with all your mind"; and, "Love your neighbor as yourself."'

"²⁸'You have answered correctly,' Jesus replied. 'Do this, and you will live.'

"²⁹But he wanted to justify himself, so he asked Jesus, 'And who is my neighbor?'

"³⁰In reply Jesus said: 'A man was going down from Jerusalem to Jericho, when he fell into the hands of robbers. They stripped him of his clothes, beat him and went away, leaving him half dead. ³¹A priest happened to be going down the same road, and when he saw the man, he passed by on the other side. ³²So too, a Levite, when he came to the place and saw him, passed by on the other side. ³³But a Samaritan, as he traveled, came where the man was; and when he saw him, he took pity on him. ³⁴He went to him and bandaged his wounds, pouring on oil and wine. Then he put the man on his own donkey, took him to an inn and took care of him. ³⁵The next day he took out two silver coins and gave them to the innkeeper. 'Look after him,' he said, 'and when I return, I will reimburse you for any extra expense you may have.'

"³⁶Which of these three do you think was a neighbor to the man who fell into the hands of robbers?' ³⁷The expert in the law replied, 'The one who had mercy on him.'

"Jesus told him, 'Go and do likewise.'"

The neighbor was _____

Jesus was asked about whom we are obligated to love as ourselves. As is often the case with Jesus, he doesn't answer his questioner outright. He

36

makes him think. Before you read further, you think, too. What is the meaning of the parable? Who is your neighbor? Who are you called to love as yourself?

It seems that Jesus didn't want limitations on whom we are to love. From the start, the lawyer's motive was wrong. Who was he really thinking about all along (see verse 29)?

Thinking about _____

Himself, of course. He wanted to justify himself. His concern was not really for his fellow man at all. His fellow man was merely a means whereby he could gain eternal life for himself. We often do things for others to relieve our own guilt or to feel better about ourselves.

When we admit to him that we cannot love others very well, and accept God's forgiving love, then we no longer have to worry about justifying ourselves or protecting ourselves. That's God's role. We receive from him the love we need to love others, and take our minds off self.

 PRAYER:
Ask God for insight as to whether this lesson rings true with you.

FOCUS:
Lord, the topic of today's lesson tells me that I need to pray before I even begin. I humbly ask for eyes to see.

Powerless to Know God's Word

What is said about man's wisdom in 1 Corinthians 1:18-25?
    "[18]For the message of the cross is foolishness to those who are perishing, but to us who are being saved it is the power of God. [19]For it is written:
    "'I will destroy the wisdom of the wise;
    "'the intelligence of the intelligent I will frustrate.'
    "[20]Where is the wise man? Where is the scholar? Where is the philosopher of this age? Has not God made foolish the wisdom of the world? [21]For since in the wisdom of God the world through its wisdom did not know him, God was pleased through the foolishness of what was preached to save those who believe. [22]Jews demand miraculous signs, and Greeks look for wisdom, [23]but we preach Christ crucified: a stumbling block to Jews and foolishness to Gentiles, [24]but to those whom God has called, both Jews and Greeks, Christ the power of God and the wisdom of God. [25]For the foolishness of God is wiser than man's wisdom, and the weakness of God is stronger than man's strength."

Do you agree or disagree with what you just read? Why or why not?

How can we understand fully the truths of God according to 2:12-16?
    "[12]We have not received the spirit of the world but the Spirit who is from God, that we may understand what God has freely given us.

38

[13]This is what we speak, not in words taught us by human wisdom but in words taught by the Spirit, expressing spiritual truths in spiritual words. [14]The man without the Spirit does not accept the things that come from the Spirit of God, for they are foolishness to him, and he cannot understand them, because they are spiritually discerned. [15]The spiritual man makes judgments about all things, but he himself is not subject to any man's judgment:

[16]"For who has known the mind of the Lord
'that he may instruct him?'
But we have the mind of Christ."

Do you see how important it is that you pray for wisdom before each time you read the Bible? Do you do so?

Not praying for insight (and expecting to get it) could lead to these feelings about reading the Word:

____ It's boring, like eating oatmeal.
____ Seems like the same old thing every time. There's nothing new.
____ I don't get anything out of it.
____ It doesn't speak to me personally.
____ I don't understand it.
____ I fall asleep.
____ I get more out of the sermons, so I'll count on those for spiritual food.

If any of these statements are your reactions to God's Word, ask yourself, "Is it because I rely on myself to get something out of the Bible, instead of asking in faith for God to visit me, teach me, speak to me?"

PRAYER:
Father, I will believe James 1:5 from now on! ("If any of you lacks wisdom, he should ask God, who gives generously to all without finding fault, and it will be given to him.")

FOCUS:
"While I draw this fleeting breath, when my eyes shall close in death, when I soar to worlds unknown, see Thee on Thy judgment throne, Rock of Ages, cleft for me, let me hide myself in Thee."

Powerless to Find Eternal Life

Thoughtfully list some of the things people do to maintain their youth and extend their life expectancy. (Examples: take vitamins, face-lift, chemotherapy)

Circle those things you do to prolong your life.

What percentage of people die?

When do you think you will die?

Are you afraid of death?

Which do you spend more time doing:

___ things that will extend your spiritual life.

___ things that will ensure eternal life.

Read John 11 and write any lessons the Holy Spirit teaches you there.

PRAYER:

Do you know you have eternal life? See verses 23 and 25-26.

"²³Jesus said to her, 'Your brother will rise again.'"

"²⁵Jesus said to her, 'I am the resurrection and the life. He who believes in me will live, even though he dies; ²⁶and whoever lives and believes in me will never die. Do you believe this?"

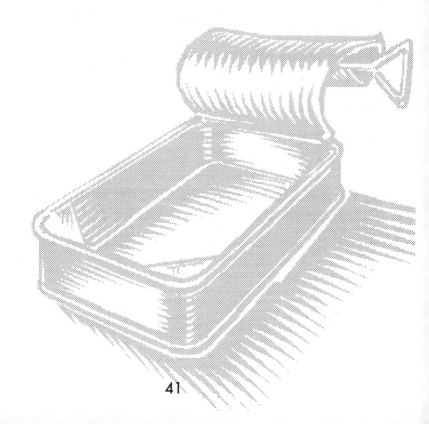

THE POWER TO CHANGE

Seeking God's Power

If you found an old oil lamp in the attic, rubbed it, and a genie popped out, offering you three wishes, what would you ask for?

Wish #1 _____

Wish #2 _____

Wish #3 _____

Would you wish for wealth, health, power or fame? Or would you lean toward asking for inner peace, good family relations, a close marriage, well-balanced children?

Jesus said, "Ask, and it will be given to you. . . . For everyone who asks receives . . . . If you, then, though you are evil, know how to give good gifts to your children, how much more will your Father in heaven give good gifts to those who ask him!" (Matthew 7:7,8,11)

The promise sounds a little genie-like. Did he mean that we can ask for *anything* and get it? Was Jesus kidding? Exaggerating? Lying?

Just think! You could have your three wishes!

But wait. Genies grant wishes indiscriminately. Even if the fulfilled wish will destroy the wisher or harm others, the genie still accommodates the wisher.

But fortunately for us, God is no genie. He gives only good gifts — gifts that are loving to us and everyone else.

One gift he wants to give us is power, real power. Power to live life to the full, to love people, to override trouble, to defeat evil, to stand above the crowd, to exalt Jesus Christ.

Is this a gift you have unwrapped? Is it a wish you've wished? Rub the lamp of God's Word this week, and see what comes out.

MONDAY

FOCUS:
Lord, there are many powers in this world. Help me not to be enticed by the weaker, easier powers, to seek after them. Rather, help me to seek you, the one true power, in all your fullness.

What powers did King Manasseh seek in 2 Kings 21:1-6?

"¹Manasseh was twelve years old when he became king, and he reigned in Jerusalem fifty-five years. His mother's name was Hephzibah. ²He did evil in the eyes of the LORD, following the detestable practices of the nations the LORD had driven out before the Israelites. ³He rebuilt the high places his father Hezekiah had destroyed; he also erected altars to Baal and made an Asherah pole, as Ahab king of Israel had done. He bowed down to all the starry hosts and worshiped them. ⁴He built altars in the temple of the LORD, of which the LORD had said, 'In Jerusalem, I will put my Name.' ⁵In both courts of the temple of the LORD, he built altars to all the starry hosts. ⁶He sacrificed his own son in the fire, practiced sorcery and divination, and consulted mediums and spiritists. He did much evil in the eyes of the LORD, provoking him to anger."

What was the reaction of the Lord?

Leviticus 20:6 reads, "I will set my face against the person who turns to mediums and spiritists to prostitute himself by following them, and I will cut him off from his people."

43

Check ✓ those things a Christian should not take part in:
- ❑ astrology/horoscopes
- ❑ palm reading/seances
- ❑ psychics/channelers
- ❑ crystals/good luck charms
- ❑ multi-religion worship services
- ❑ chanting/mantras

Circle the ugly "P" word used in Leviticus 20:6 to describe what we do when we turn to such things for help.

The Bible teaches we are all married to one husband, the Lord. To seek spiritual power or insight from another source is to commit spiritual adultery. God alone should be (and is) enough.

"For us there is but one God, the Father, from whom all things came and for whom we live; and there is but one Lord, Jesus Christ, through whom all things came and through whom we live."
(1 Corinthians 8:6)

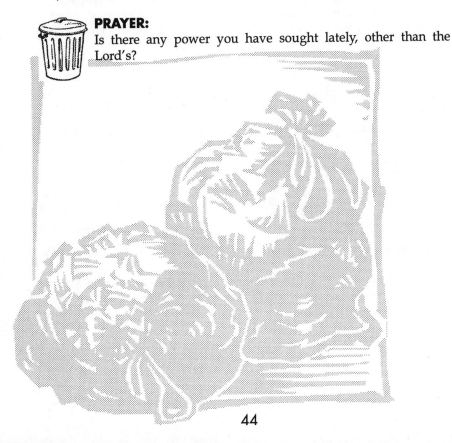

PRAYER:
Is there any power you have sought lately, other than the Lord's?

44

 FOCUS:
Confess to the Lord that he is the only power you need.

There are many ways to try to gain power, influence or victory in this world. What methods should we not rely upon, according to each of these verses?

1 Samuel 16:6-7 _____

_____

Psalm 146:3-4 _____

_____

Jeremiah 9:23-24 _____

_____

1 Corinthians 1:22-23 _____

_____

What do you tend to rely on for personal success?

❏   beauty/figure/looks
❏   people/family/spouse
❏   money/position/possessions
❏   strength/physique/athleticism
❏   brains/knowledge/education

Paraphrase what Paul says in 1 Corinthians 2:1-5.

"¹When I came to you, brothers, I did not come with eloquence or superior wisdom as I proclaimed to you the testimony about God. ²For I resolved to know nothing while I was with you except Jesus Christ and him crucified. ³I came to you in weakness and fear, and with much trembling. ⁴My message and my preaching were not with wise and persuasive words, but with a demonstration of the Spirit's power, ⁵so that your faith might not rest on men's wisdom, but on God's power."

My paraphrase:

_____
_____
_____
_____
_____

Where does your faith rest in each of the following arenas of your life?

➤ salvation _____

➤ love life _____

➤ parenting _____

➤ business _____

➤ self-esteem _____

➤ happiness _____

PRAYER:
Examine yourself before the Lord.

WEDNESDAY

FOCUS:
Who or what was your primary power yesterday?

Today we look at seeking God's power in God's way, not our own fashion. What do you learn from King Saul's folly in 1 Samuel 13:1-15?

"¹Saul was thirty years old when he became king, and he reigned over Israel forty-two years.

"²Saul chose three thousand men from Israel; two thousand were with him at Micmash and in the hill country of Bethel, and a thousand were with Jonathan at Gibeah in Benjamin. The rest of the men he sent back to their homes.

"³Jonathan attacked the Philistine outpost at Geba, and the Philistines heard about it. Then Saul had the trumpet blown throughout the land and said, 'Let the Hebrews hear!' ⁴So all Israel heard the news: 'Saul has attacked the Philistine outpost, and now Israel has become a stench to the Philistines.' And the people were summoned to join Saul at Gilgal.

"⁵The Philistines assembled to fight Israel, with three thousand chariots, six thousand charioteers, and soldiers as numerous as the sand on the seashore. They went up and camped at Micmash, east of Beth Aven. ⁶When the men of Israel saw that their situation was critical and that their army was hard pressed, they hid in caves and thickets, among the rocks, and in pits and cisterns. ⁷Some Hebrews even crossed the Jordan to the land of Gad and Gilead.

"Saul remained at Gilgal, and all the troops with him were quaking with fear. ⁸He waited seven days, the time set by Samuel; but Samuel did not come to Gilgal, and Saul's men began to scatter. ⁹So he said, 'Bring me the burnt offering and the fellowship offerings.' And Saul offered up the burnt offering. ¹⁰Just as he finished making the offering, Samuel arrived, and Saul went out to greet him.

"¹¹'What have you done?' asked Samuel.

"Saul replied, 'When I saw that the men were scattering and that you did not come at the set time, and that the Philistines were assembling at Micmash, ¹²I thought, 'Now the Philistines will come down against me at Gilgal, and I have not sought the LORD's favor.' So I felt compelled to offer the burnt offering.'

"¹³'You acted foolishly,' Samuel said. 'You have not kept the command the LORD your God gave you; if you had, he would have established your kingdom over Israel for all time. [14]But now your kingdom will not endure; the LORD has sought out a man after his own heart and appointed him leader of his people, because you have not kept the LORD's command.'

"[15]Then Samuel left Gilgal and went up to Gibeah in Benjamin, and Saul counted the men who were with him. They numbered about six hundred."

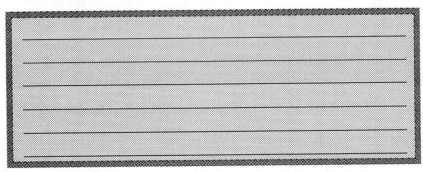

Saul was not allowed to sacrifice. Instead of trusting the Lord to come through as he had promised through the always reliable prophet Samuel, Saul took matters into his own hands. When you study Saul's life, you see that his primary concern was for his own reputation. He was not out to glorify the Lord, but to save his kingly name.

Throughout Scripture, we are given these principles in using God's power: 1) wait on God, even when it looks bleak; 2) obey, even when it seems unreasonable; and 3) do it for his glory, then he, in turn, will glorify you.

In which of the following areas do you do well? Underline them. In which do you need work? Circle them.

WAITING: for the right mate, for sex in marriage, for the "big" assignment, for answers to prayer, for healing, for daily strength.

OBEYING: praying, reading the Word, keeping pure, forgiving offenses, putting others first.

GLORIFYING: thinking of God's reputation before your own, deflecting the credit to him, praising him at church and home.

PRAYER:
To you, Lord, be the glory, honor and power forever. Amen.

THURSDAY

FOCUS:
Lord, show me your power today. Help me not to fear it or distrust it, but rather to expect it and count on it.

What were the disciples told to wait on in Acts 1:3-9?

"³After his suffering, he showed himself to these men and gave many convincing proofs that he was alive. He appeared to them over a period of forty days and spoke about the kingdom of God. ⁴On one occasion, while he was eating with them, he gave them this command: 'Do not leave Jerusalem, but wait for the gift my Father promised, which you have heard me speak about. ⁵For John baptized with water, but in a few days you will be baptized with the Holy Spirit.'

"⁶So when they met together, they asked him, 'Lord, are you at this time going to restore the kingdom to Israel?'

"⁷He said to them: 'It is not for you to know the times or dates the Father has set by his own authority. ⁸But you will receive power when the Holy Spirit comes on you; and you will be my witnesses in Jerusalem, and in all Judea and Samaria, and to the ends of the earth.'

"⁹After he said this, he was taken up before their very eyes, and a cloud hid him from their sight."

What were they empowered to do in Acts 2:1-14?

"¹When the day of Pentecost came, they were all together in one place. ²Suddenly a sound like the blowing of a violent wind came from heaven and filled the whole house where they were sitting. ³They saw what seemed to be tongues of fire that separated and came to rest on each of them. ⁴All of them were filled with the Holy Spirit and began to speak in other tongues as the Spirit enabled them.

"⁵Now there were staying in Jerusalem God-fearing Jews from every nation under heaven. ⁶When they heard this sound, a crowd came together in bewilderment, because each one heard them

49

speaking in his own language. ⁷Utterly amazed, they asked: 'Are not all these men who are speaking Galileans? ⁸Then how is it that each of us hears them in his own native language? ⁹Parthians, Medes and Elamites; residents of Mesopotamia, Judea and Cappadocia, Pontus and Asia, ¹⁰Phyrgia and Pamphylia, Egypt and the part of Libya near Cyrene; visitors from Rome ¹¹(both Jews and converts to Judaism); Cretans and Arabs — we hear them declaring the wonders of God in our own tongues!' ¹²Amazed and perplexed, they asked one another, 'What does this mean?'

"¹³Some, however, made fun of them and said, 'They have had too much wine.'

"¹⁴Then Peter stood up with the Eleven, raised his voice and addressed the crowd: 'Fellow Jews and all of you who live in Jerusalem, let me explain this to you; listen carefully to what I say.'"

_____

_____

_____

The important truth is not that the disciples could speak in foreign languages but that they were enabled to powerfully preach Christ, so fulfilling the great commission. The focus is not on tongues, but on Jesus.

Answer these questions from Acts 2:38. ("Peter replied, 'Repent and be baptized, every one of you, in the name of Jesus Christ for the forgiveness of your sins. And you will receive the gift of the Holy Spirit.'")

Who can have this Holy Spirit?

_____

The Spirit is promised to those who do what?

____ repent
____ pray for several hours
____ are baptized in the name of Jesus
____ live perfect lives

The Holy Spirit is . . .

____ earned by good works
____ received as a gift
____ only for some Christians

50

Do you have the Holy Spirit, based on Acts 2:38?

How do you know?

_____

_____

_____

Where do you see the Holy Spirit at work in your life? Name three places:

1. _____

2. _____

3. _____

PRAYER:
Thank you for your Holy Spirit in me.

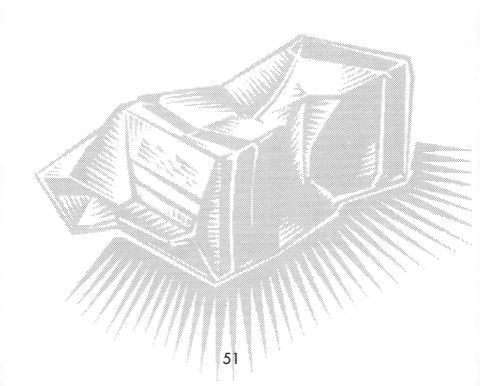

FRIDAY

FOCUS:
Thank you that your holy presence continues in me.

What will the Holy Spirit do in and through you, according to these Scriptures?

Matthew 10:18-20 _____

_____

John 14:26 _____

_____

John 16:7-8 _____

_____

Romans 5:5 _____

_____

Romans 8:13 _____

_____

Romans 8:15, 26-27 _____

_____

Romans 8:16 _____

_____

In which areas do you see him at work now? Circle them, and thank God for it.

In which areas do you not see the Spirit at work in you? He wants to be active in each of these ways in you. What is the reason he isn't? Do you not trust him to be working in you? Are you afraid of the effect he might have? Have you been ignorant that he wants to do that?

If you are willing, pray this prayer to close our study this week:

Lord, I thank you for the promised Holy Spirit — your power given to us as a gift. I thank you that I have experienced his power in these ways:

_____

_____

I also confess I have not experienced your Spirit in these ways:

_____

_____

I ask you humbly to fill me with every facet of your Spirit, so that I might do your work in this world. For Jesus' sake, Amen.

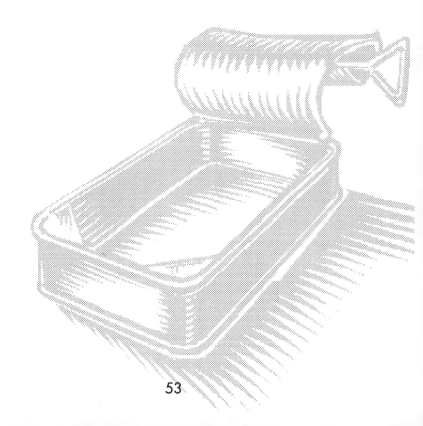

THE VERDICT IS GUILTY!

From Sin to Forgiveness

Several attitudes can keep us from experiencing the full forgiveness, cleansing and freedom God wants us to have:

1. "I don't think I am much of a sinner."
2. "I don't deserve forgiveness. God won't forgive me."
3. "I believe God forgives me, but I can't forgive myself."

Each of these beliefs restrains divine cleansing. Here's how:

1. You cannot be forgiven for things for which you do not ask forgiveness. Forgiveness demands two things: confession and repentance.

   If we do not admit our wrongs, or only admit those most painless and convenient to admit, then our sense of relief will be small.

2. Although Jesus Christ has died to secure our pardon, we must accept it. Even a free gift, if left untouched and unused, is of no use. Having the cure for our sickness doesn't help; it is trusting and taking the medicine that heals us.

3. We don't really experience forgiveness if we can't forgive ourselves. Furthermore, we are in rebellion to God, putting ourselves on the judgment seat where only he belongs. We believe, in essence, that our judgment is more righteous than God's. Saying, "I can't forgive myself" may appear humble and righteous, but in truth it is rebellious and prideful. We set ourselves up as judge and jury. But the Bible clearly says there is one Judge. Accept his verdict this week.

MONDAY

FOCUS:
Lord, help me today to put your X-ray machine up to my heart, and be open to finding any unbecoming, undesirable spot or corruption in me.

How good are you? Where would you place yourself on this righteousness scale?

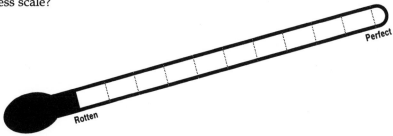

Perfect

Rotten

How bad does the Bible indicate the woman mentioned in Luke 7:36-50 was?

"³⁶Now one of the Pharisees invited Jesus to have dinner with him, so he went to the Pharisee's house and reclined at the table. ³⁷When a woman who had lived a sinful life in that town learned that Jesus was eating at the Pharisee's house, she brought an alabaster jar of perfume, ³⁸and as she stood behind him at his feet weeping, she began to wet his feet with her tears. Then she wiped them with her hair, kissed them and poured perfume on them.

"³⁹When the Pharisee who had invited him saw this, he said to himself, 'If this man were a prophet, he would know who is touching him and what kind of woman she is — that she is a sinner.'

"⁴⁰Jesus answered him, 'Simon, I have something to tell you.'

"'Tell me, teacher,' he said.

"⁴¹'Two men owed money to a certain moneylender. One owed him five hundred denarii, and the other fifty. ⁴²Neither of them had the money to pay him back, so he canceled the debts of both. Now which of them will love him more?'

"⁴³Simon replied, 'I suppose the one who had the bigger debt canceled.'

"'You have judged correctly,' Jesus said.

"⁴⁴Then he turned toward the woman and said to Simon, 'Do you see this woman? I came into your house. You did not give me any water for my feet, but she wet my feet with her tears and wiped

55

them with her hair. "You did not give me a kiss, but this woman, from the time I entered, has not stopped kissing my feet. "You did not put oil on my head, but she has poured perfume on my feet. "Therefore, I tell you, her many sins have been forgiven — for she loved much. But he who has been forgiven little loves little.'

"⁴⁸Then Jesus said to her, 'Your sins are forgiven.'

"⁴⁹The other guests began to say among themselves, 'Who is this who even forgives sins?'

"⁵⁰Jesus said to the woman, 'Your faith has saved you; go in peace.'"

From what you read, how bad did she see herself to be, in one word:

_____

List everything she did that shows you that she knew herself to be a sinner and was repentant:

_____

_____

_____

Now compare (or contrast) yourself with the woman. Name three ways you are alike or different:

1. _____

2. _____

3. _____

What word does Jesus use to describe the woman after her repentance (verses 47-48)?

_____

What word in verse 50?

_____

PRAYER:
Do these words describe you? If so, are you willing to do what this woman did?

 FOCUS:
"Search me, O God, and know my heart; test me and know my anxious thoughts. See if there is any offensive way in me, and lead me in the way everlasting." (Psalm 139:23-24)

Read Luke 7:36-50 again and write below everything you find that the Pharisee did, thought, and said.

_____

_____

_____

In a word, describe the Pharisee. _____

How are you like or unlike him?

1. _____

2. _____

3. _____

If you are having trouble comparing yourself to the man, see if you have any of the following beliefs. (Be honest! Remember, the Lord is watching.)

❏ I have invited Jesus to my "house" as a guest, too.

❏ I need some forgiveness, but not a whole lot.

❏ I appreciate Jesus.

❏ My sins are mostly small ones.

❏ I think I am better than some people, probably most people.

❏ My sins deserve some punishment, but not too much.

Which of the "sinful woman's" attitude do you have?

❏ I have invited Jesus in as my Lord and King.

❏ I am in desperate need of forgiveness.

- ❏ I adore Jesus.
- ❏ I am the "worst of sinners."
- ❏ I deserve death for my sins.

 PRAYER:
Ask the Lord his opinion on who you are more like — the woman or the Pharisee.

FOCUS:
"God, have mercy on me, a sinner." (Luke 18:13)

What is the meaning of Jesus' parable in Luke 7:41-43?

"⁴¹Two men owed money to a certain moneylender. One owed him five hundred denarii, and the other fifty. ⁴²Neither of them had the money to pay him back, so he canceled the debts of both. Now which of them will love him more?

"⁴³Simon replied, 'I suppose the one who had the bigger debt canceled.'

"'You have judged correctly,' Jesus said."

_____

_____

_____

Of how much have you been forgiven: Ten sins? 100? 1,000? One million? How much would your debt of sin be by the end of your life if you only sinned five times daily?

> 365 days per year × 5 sins per day
>
> = _____ (subtotal)
>
> × 70 years of life
>
> = _____ Grand Total

We usually grade ourselves leniently. We excuse our wrong actions (or inactions), exaggerate our good deeds, and ignore some commands outright, because they are just too hard. Paul wrote that any action that does not arise from faith is sin. Jesus said it is not just our actions that can be sinful, but also our attitudes and motivations as well. Matthew 5:48 says, "Be perfect, therefore, as you heavenly Father is perfect."

With this in mind, read the list of biblical dos and don'ts, then estimate how many times you come up short on an average day.

DON'T . . . lie, lust, steal, hate, fear, worry, kill, cheat, ridicule, call names, boast, covet, or complain.

DO . . . love God with all your heart, soul, mind and strength; love your neighbor as yourself; give self up for others; forgive all; give generously; hate evil; visit the sick; pray continuously; rejoice in all circumstances; seek first the kingdom of God; boldly witness.

DO

‾‾‾‾‾‾‾‾‾‾

DON'T

‾‾‾‾‾‾‾‾‾‾

PRAYER:
God, have mercy on me, a sinner.

THURSDAY

FOCUS:
"Holy, holy, holy is the Lord God Almighty, who was, and is, and is to come." (Revelation 4:8)

Yesterday you estimated how many times a day you come up short of God's plan for your life. Now estimate how many sins you have committed so far in your life.

> 365 days per year
>
> × _____ your estimated sins per day
>
> = _____ (subtotal)
>
> × _____ years since you came of accountable age
>
> = _____ Your Grand Total

Read about three times people met God in his holiness. What were their responses?

Isaiah 6:1-8
    "¹In the year that King Uzziah died, I saw the Lord seated on a throne, high and exalted, and the train of his robe filled the temple. ²Above him were seraphs, each with six wings: With two wings they covered their faces, with two they covered their feet, and with two they were flying. ³And they were calling to one another:
    "'Holy, holy, holy is the LORD Almighty; the whole earth is full of his glory.' ⁴At the sound of their voices the doorposts and thresholds shook and the temple was filled with smoke.
    "'⁵Woe to me!' I cried. 'I am ruined! For I am a man of unclean lips, and I live among a people of unclean lips, and my eyes have seen the King, the LORD Almighty.'
    "'⁶Then one of the seraphs flew to me with a live coal in his hand, which he had taken with tongs from the altar. ⁷With it he touched my mouth and said, 'See, this has touched your lips; your guilt is taken away and your sin atoned for.'
    "'⁸Then I heard the voice of the Lord saying, 'Whom shall I send? And who will go for us?'
    "And I said, 'Here am I. Send me!'"

_____

_____

Ezekiel 1:26-28

"²⁶Above the expanse over their heads was what looked like a throne of sapphire, and high above on the throne was a figure like that of a man. ²⁷I saw that from what appeared to be his waist up he looked like glowing metal, as if full of fire, and that from there down he looked like fire; and brilliant light surrounded him. ²⁸Like the appearance of a rainbow in the clouds on a rainy day, so was the radiance around him."

Revelation 1:9-18

"⁹I, John, your brother and companion in the suffering and kingdom and patient endurance that are ours in Jesus, was on the island of Patmos because of the word of God and the testimony of Jesus. ¹⁰On the Lord's Day I was in the Spirit, and I heard behind me a loud voice like a trumpet, ¹¹which said: 'Write on a scroll what you see and send it to the seven churches: to Ephesus, Smyrna, Pergamum, Thyatira, Sardis, Philadelphia and Laodicea.'

¹²I turned around to see the voice that was speaking to me. And when I turned I saw seven golden lampstands, ¹³and among the lampstands was someone 'like a son of man,' dressed in a robe reaching down to his feet and with a golden sash around his chest. ¹⁴His head and hair were white like wool, as white as snow, and his eyes were like blazing fire. ¹⁵His feet were like bronze glowing in a furnace, and his voice was like the sound of rushing waters. ¹⁶In his right hand he held seven stars, and out of his mouth came a sharp double-edged sword. His face was like the sun shining in all its brilliance.

¹⁷When I saw him, I fell at his feet as though dead. Then he placed his right hand on me and said: 'Do not be afraid. I am the First and the Last. ¹⁸I am the Living One; I was dead, and behold I am alive for ever and ever! And I hold the keys of death and Hades.'"

Have you done what these men did? If not, will you do it now?

Over and over the Bible teaches "humble yourselves before the Lord and he will lift you up." Notice what the Lord did after each man fell before him:

Isaiah 6:7 — "See, this has touched your lips; your guilt is taken away and your sin atoned for."

Ezekiel 2:2 — "As he spoke, the Spirit came into me and raised me to my feet."

Revelation 1:17 — "Then he placed his right hand on me and said, 'Do not be afraid.'"

God lifts and forgives the humble and contrite. "A broken and contrite heart, O God, you will not despise." (Psalm 51:17)

PRAYER:
Use Psalm 32:1-6 as the basis for your prayer.

"¹Blessed is he whose transgressions are forgiven, whose sins are covered. ²Blessed is the man whose sin the LORD does not count against him and in whose spirit is no deceit.

"³When I kept silent, my bones wasted away through my groaning all day long. ⁴For day and night your hand was heavy upon me; my strength was sapped as in the heat of summer. ⁵Then I acknowledged my sin to you and did not cover up my iniquity. I said, 'I will confess my transgressions to the LORD' — and you forgave the guilt of my sin. ⁶Therefore let everyone who is godly pray to you while you may be found; surely when the mighty waters rise, they will not reach him."

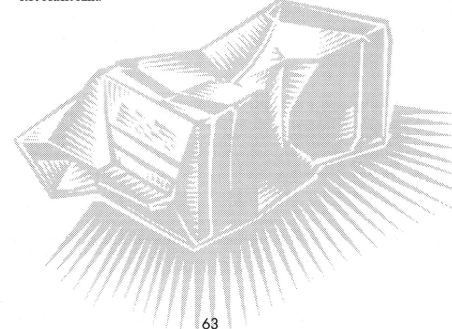

FRIDAY

FOCUS:

"If you, O LORD, kept a record of sins, O Lord, who could stand? But with you there is forgiveness; therefore you are feared." (Psalm 130:3-4)

Many people can believe they are forgiven for most of their sins, but not quite all. There are a select few too awful to be cleansed. They believe that God forgives, but they can't forgive themselves. Search your past. Are there sins you still hold guilt over? Sex before marriage, an abortion, the time you embarrassed your family, a poorly reared child?

Read Isaiah 53 and choose three phrases that stand out to you, writing them in the box at the end.

"¹Who has believed our message and to whom has the arm of the LORD been revealed? ²He grew up before him like a tender shoot, and like a root out of dry ground. He had no beauty or majesty to attract us to him, nothing in his appearance that we should desire him. ³He was despised and rejected by men, a man of sorrows, and familiar with suffering. Like one from whom men hide their faces he was despised, and we esteemed him not.

"⁴Surely he took up our infirmities and carried our sorrows, yet we considered him stricken by God, smitten by him, and afflicted. ⁵But he was pierced for our transgressions, he was crushed for our iniquities; the punishment that brought us peace was upon him, and by his wounds we are healed. ⁶We all, like sheep, have gone astray, each of us has turned to his own way; and the LORD has laid on him the iniquity of us all.

"⁷He was oppressed and afflicted, yet he did not open his mouth; he was led like a lamb to the slaughter, and as a sheep before her shearers is silent, so he did not open his mouth. ⁸By oppression and judgment he was taken away. And who can speak of his descendants? For he was cut off from the land of the living; for the transgression of my people he was stricken. ⁹He was assigned a grave

64

with the wicked, and with the rich in his death, though he had done no violence, nor was any deceit in his mouth.

"¹⁰Yet it was the LORD's will to crush him and cause him to suffer, and though the LORD makes his life a guilt offering, he will see his offspring and prolong his days, and the will of the LORD will prosper in his hand.

"¹¹After the suffering of his soul, he will see the light of life and be satisfied; by his knowledge my righteous servant will justify many, and he will bear their iniquities. ¹²Therefore I will give him a portion among the great, and he will divide the spoils with the strong, because he poured out his life unto death, and was numbered with the transgressors. For he bore the sin of many, and made intercession for the transgressors."

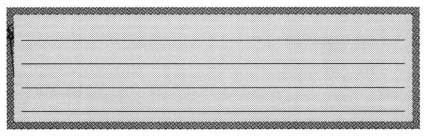

Can you, by faith, believe that every shortcoming, every ugly action, every wrong thought of yours is blotted out and forgiven by Jesus' death for you? If so, draw a cross over the sins you listed on page 64.

Look back to Monday's devotion. See the things you wrote about the woman's repentance. With all Jesus has done for you, can you see yourself doing what this woman did? If not, maybe you still fear Jesus doesn't love you or are still not convicted by the depth of your sin and the height of his sacrifice.

 PRAYER:
Read Psalm 51:1-17 out loud as your closing prayer. Reading aloud can make prayer more powerful to you.

"¹Have mercy on me, O God, according to your unfailing love; according to your great compassion blot out my transgressions. ²Wash away all my iniquity and cleanse me from my sin.

"³For I know my transgressions, and my sin is always before me. ⁴Against you, you only, have I sinned and done what is evil in your sight, so that you are proved right when you speak and justified when you judge. ⁵Surely I was sinful at birth, sinful from the time my mother conceived me. ⁶Surely you desire truth in the inner parts; you teach me wisdom in the inmost place.

"⁷Cleanse me with hyssop, and I will be clean; wash me, and I will be whiter than snow. ⁸Let me hear joy and gladness; let the bones you have crushed rejoice. ⁹Hide your face from my sins and blot out all my iniquity.

"¹⁰Create in me a pure heart, O God, and renew a steadfast spirit within me. ¹¹Do not cast me from your presence or take your Holy Spirit from me. ¹²Restore to me the joy of your salvation and grant me a willing spirit, to sustain me.

"¹³Then I will teach transgressors your ways, and sinners will turn back to you. ¹⁴Save me from bloodguilt, O God, the God who saves me, and my tongue will sing of your righteousness. ¹⁵O Lord, open my lips, and my mouth will declare your praise. ¹⁶You do not delight in sacrifice, or I would bring it; you do not take pleasure in burnt offerings. ¹⁷The sacrifices of God are a broken spirit; a broken and contrite heart, O God, you will not despise.

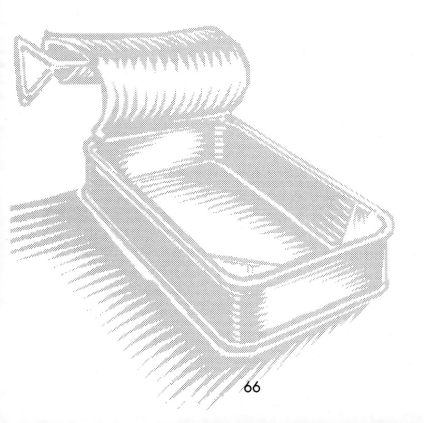

66

HE CHANGED ME!

Taking a Different Road

What is your reaction to this prayer: "Lord, give me clarity of vision that will save me from mistaking . . .

> . . . a busy life for a fruitful life
> . . . success for faithfulness
> . . . the praise of people for the praise of God
> . . . organization for inspiration
> . . . facility of speech for spiritual power
> . . . laziness for rest
> . . . planning for praying
> . . . head knowledge for heart experiences."

It seems so easy to fall into the rut of worldly thinking and cheap values, while eternal appointments go unmet. We often do the easy things, the expected things, the habitual things the immediate-gratification things, the things we have always done, rather than the eternal things, the character things, the Christ things.

But Jesus shows us again what is important. This man who never had a two-car garage, a six-figure salary, a vacation house on the lake, or a nameplate on his office door, died and rose from the dead, and impacted the world more than all the philosophers, executives, superstars and presidents of all ages combined.

Jesus was a real man. A true man. A right man.

And he says to you, "Come follow me."

Are you following?

Who are you more like? John Wayne or Jesus Christ? Your earthly dad or your heavenly Father? Everyone else or the One and Only?

Be different. Be transformed. Be resurrected. Be like Christ!

MONDAY

FOCUS:
Offer up the petition from the introduction to the devotion.

This week we will look at five requirements for personal transformation.

#1 — Believe God loves you and wants the best for you.

This truth may seem elementary, but most Christians are not 100 percent convinced of its veracity. The true believer has no trouble saying, "God, your will be done in my life, no matter what it is — even sending me to Africa or Asia as a missionary, even witnessing to my boss, even teaching a youth class — whatever, because I know you love me and will perform the best for me!"

We have difficulty trusting God's love totally because we have been hurt, even when trying to do what God wanted. Down deep, we begin to think, "It's better to rely on and protect myself; I don't know if God will come through."

But God never promised to give us an easy life, only the *best* life. "Easy" and "best" never go together, any more than do "easy" and "champion" or "easy" and "love."

Read John chapters 17, 18 and 19 and list some of the ways Jesus proved he loves you and wants the best for you.

PRAYER:
If you have doubted that God loves you and wants the best for you, that he is wholly reliable, confess that sin to God, openly, aloud.

TUESDAY

FOCUS:
Thank you, Father, for loving me and all people to the highest heaven and the lowest valley.

Our second transforming truth is:

**#2 — Believe your every sin is forgiven
and you are free from the slavery of guilt.**

Rummage through your closet. Is there anything for which you still feel guilty, still carry around sin's weight like a sack of rotten potatoes, can't shake loose the sense of failure?

Many people think God wants them to feel guilty; that God likes it when folks carry guilt because it keeps them humble, and in their place.

Do you believe God is pleased with your guilt? That he is glad when you are miserable with sin's weight? ❑ Yes ❑ No

Let's say you felt free from the guilt of sin. What do you think God's reaction would be to that, in one word?

God is most glorified when we are alive, joyful, free, energized by his presence. When we continue to feel guilt, then we are afraid to approach him confidently and are not in close relationship with him. Guilt-ridden Christians make poor examples of what God wants to do for his world. What do these passages tell you?

Hebrews 4:15-16
"[15]For we do not have a high priest who is unable to sympathize with our weaknesses, but we have one who has been tempted in every way, just as we are — yet was without sin. [16]Let us then approach the throne of grace with confidence, so that we may receive mercy and find grace to help us in our time of need."

Hebrews 9:14

"[14]'How much more, then, will the blood of Christ, who through the eternal Spirit offered himself unblemished to God, cleanse our consciences from acts that lead to death, so that we may serve the living God!'"

Hebrews 10:22-23

"[22]Let us draw near to God with a sincere heart in full assurance of faith, having our hearts sprinkled to cleanse us from a guilty conscience and having our bodies washed with pure water. [23]Let us hold unswervingly to the hope we profess, for he who promised is faithful.'"

---

1 John 3:19-22

"[19]This then is how we know that we belong to the truth, and how we set our hearts at rest in his presence [20]whenever our hearts condemn us. For God is greater than our hearts, and he knows everything.

"[21]Dear friends, if our hearts do not condemn us, we have confidence before God [22]and receive from him anything we ask, because we obey his commands and do what pleases him.'"

If you were totally free from a guilty conscience, how would your life be different?

_____

_____

_____

Would this change glorify God or defame him?

 PRAYER:
Thy will be done in my forgiveness.

WEDNESDAY

Our next requirement is:

#3 — Put away every idol.

We no longer carve wood or fashion stone into a likeness, then fall down and worship it. We are too sophisticated for that. But that doesn't stop us from idol worship!

An idol is anything we look to, hoping it will give us what only God can give — value, meaning, significance, purpose, hope, life, happiness.

Have you noticed that Jesus often asked people to leave behind every visible means of support, and follow him?

What would you say were Paul's idols before coming to Christ? Read Philippians 3:1-11.

"[1]Finally, my brothers, rejoice in the Lord! It is no trouble for me to write the same things to you again, and it is a safeguard for you.

"[2]Watch out for those dogs, those men who do evil, those mutilators of the flesh. [3]For it is we who are the circumcision, we who worship by the Spirit of God, who glory in Christ Jesus, and who put no confidence in the flesh — [4]though I myself have reasons for such confidence.

"If anyone else thinks he has reasons to put confidence in the flesh, I have more: [5]circumcised on the eighth day, of the people of Israel, of the tribe of Benjamin, a Hebrew of Hebrews; in regard to the law, a Pharisee; [6]as for zeal, persecuting the church; as for legalistic righteousness, faultless.

"[7]But whatever was to my profit I now consider loss for the sake of Christ. [8]What is more, I consider everything a loss compared to the surpassing greatness of knowing Christ Jesus my Lord, for whose sake I have lost all things. I consider them rubbish, that I may gain Christ [9]and be found in him, not having a righteousness of my own that comes from the law, but that which is through faith in Christ — the righteousness that comes from God and is by faith. [10]I want to know Christ and the power of his resurrection and the fellowship of sharing in his sufferings, becoming like him in his death, "and so, somehow, to attain to the resurrection from the dead."

_____

_____

_____

Would you feel more important, acceptable, worthwhile, content, safe or confident if you . . .

- ❑ lost 30 pounds
- ❑ were promoted at work
- ❑ bought a new car or truck
- ❑ had a golf score in the 70s
- ❑ were married
- ❑ had a boat on the river
- ❑ wore expensive, sexy clothes
- ❑ were funny, the life of the party
- ❑ were not divorced
- ❑ had a house in a prestigious neighborhood
- ❑ were well-known in your field
- ❑ had money to do what you want
- ❑ could sing in front of large audiences
- ❑ were loved by everybody

Could any of these be an idol?

 PRAYER:
Father, I will count on you alone to give me meaning, purpose, importance, significance and value. I reject these idols. You are enough for me.

THURSDAY

FOCUS:
Thank you that all I need to be "somebody" is to know the One and Only.

Today's necessity for transformation is:

#4 — Stop relying on your own power, and trust God's transformation.

We often believe that we must do it all ourselves. We think that God is pleased when we work hard. What should be the power in a Christian's life, according to these verses?

John 15:4-5
"⁴Remain in me, and I will remain in you. No branch can bear fruit by itself; it must remain in the vine. Neither can you bear fruit unless you remain in me.

"⁵I am the vine; you are the branches. If a man remains in me and I in him, he will bear much fruit; apart from me you can do nothing.'"

1 Corinthians 15:10
"¹⁰But by the grace of God I am what I am, and his grace to me was not without effect. No, I worked harder than all of them — yet not I, but the grace of God that was with me."

Ephesians 2:10
"¹⁰For we are God's workmanship, created in Christ Jesus to do good works, which God prepared in advance for us to do."

Philippians 2:12-13
"¹²Therefore, my dear friends, as you have always obeyed — not only in my presence, but now much more in my absence — continue to work out your salvation with fear and trembling, ¹³for it is God who works in you to will and to act according to his good purpose."

Colossians 1:28-29

"²⁸We proclaim him, admonishing and teaching everyone with all wisdom, so that we may present everyone perfect in Christ. ²⁹To this end I labor, struggling with all his energy, which so powerfully works in me."

✓ Check each verse if you really believe it. ✓ Check it again if you really live by it!

Read Luke 24, noting anything that demonstrates Jesus Christ's power.

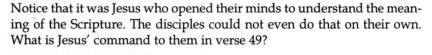

Notice that it was Jesus who opened their minds to understand the meaning of the Scripture. The disciples could not even do that on their own. What is Jesus' command to them in verse 49?

PRAYER:
Do you have this power? (See Acts 2:38 — Peter replied, "Repent and be baptized, every one of you, in the name of Jesus Christ for the forgiveness of your sins. And you will receive the gift of the Holy Spirit.") If so, do you expect it to work in your life daily? Do you humbly depend on it, or only call on God in a scrape?

FOCUS:
Praise God for his power at work in you.

Our last key to a transformed life is:

#5 — Live by his Word, not your ideas.

Here is another simple rule that is often agreed to mentally but ignored in actuality.

Answer these three questions:

1. Who are the authorities in this world? _____

2. What is your goal in life? _____

3. What do you fear? _____

Read Matthew 28, another account of the resurrection.

"[1]After the Sabbath, at dawn on the first day of the week, Mary Magdalene and the other Mary went to look at the tomb.

"[2]There was a violent earthquake, for an angel of the Lord came down from heaven and, going to the tomb, rolled back the stone and sat on it. [3]His appearance was like lightning, and his clothes were white as snow. [4]The guards were so afraid of him that they shook and became like dead men.

"[5]The angel said to the women, 'Do not be afraid, for I know that you are looking for Jesus, who was crucified. [6]He is not here; he has risen, just as he said. Come and see the place where he lay. [7]Then go quickly and tell his disciples: "He has risen from the dead and is going ahead of you into Galilee. There you will see him." Now I have told you.'

"[8]So the women hurried away from the tomb, afraid yet filled with joy, and ran to tell his disciples. [9]Suddenly Jesus met them. 'Greetings,' he said. They came to him, clasped his feet and worshiped him. [10]Then Jesus said to them, 'Do not be afraid. Go and tell my brothers to go to Galilee; there they will see me.'

"[11]While the women were on their way, some of the guards went into the city and reported to the chief priests everything that had happened. [12]When the chief priests had met with the elders and devised a plan, they gave the soldiers a large sum of money, [13]telling them, 'You are to say, 'His disciples came during the night and stole him away while we were asleep.' [14]If this report gets to the governor, we will satisfy him and keep you out of trouble.' [15]So the soldiers took the money and did as they were instructed. And this story has been widely circulated among the Jews to this very day.

"[16]Then the eleven disciples went to Galilee, to the mountain where Jesus had told them to go. [17]When they saw him, they worshiped him; but some doubted. [18]Then Jesus came to them and said, 'All authority in heaven and on earth has been given to me. [19]Therefore go and make disciples of all nations, baptizing them in the name of the Father and of the Son and of the Holy Spirit, [20]and teaching them to obey everything I have commanded you. And surely I am with you always, to the very end of the age.'"

Write here everything Jesus said in that passage.

_____

_____

_____

_____

Answer the first three questions once more, based on what Jesus says.

1. _____

2. _____

3. _____

If a person really believed wholly in the resurrection of Jesus and in his own life after death, and he believed in heaven and rewards and the fact that 70 years is a drop in the bucket when viewed from eternity, and that he will really see Jesus face-to-face someday, how would such a person live? List five things he would do regularly.

1. _____

_____

2. _____

_____

3. _____

_____

4. _____

_____

5. _____

_____

 PRAYER:
Father, help me to say, like Paul, "To live is Christ and to die is gain" (Philippians 1:21).

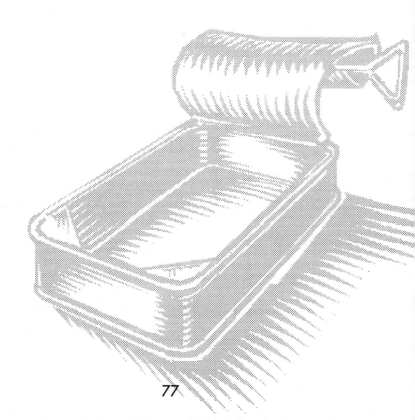

SOMETHING MUCH MORE

The Reality of the Holy Spirit

The Bible teaches that, as humans, we operate on three levels: body, soul and spirit. Preacher Stuart Briscoe says it is possible for us to operate on all three levels or just as possible to function on only one or two. For example, when a person's physical body dies, his soul lives on.

Briscoe writes in *Transforming the Daily Grind*, "If you are reading this, you are most certainly physically alive. But do not assume that you are necessarily spiritually alive, for it is quite possible that you could be reading this and be dead."

He cites in 1 Timothy 5:6, "The widow who lives for pleasure is dead even while she lives." Jesus said, "I have come that they may have life," that is, so physically alive men who are spiritually dead may come alive in a new way.

Briscoe lists three signs of life:

1. Appetite. Physically dead men don't eat or even want to. Spiritually dead men have no appetite for God's Word.

2. Activity. Physically dead men don't do anything. Spiritually dead men can't find time to do anything for the church.

3. Awareness. Physically dead men aren't cognizant of those around them or of what's going on. The spiritually dead are unaware of God's presence and voice. They never hear him.

Speaker Tommy Oaks talks of Lazarus from John 11 in this way. "Lazarus had money. He was rich! Lazarus had possessions. He was comfortable! Lazarus had friends. He was popular! Lazarus only had one problem. HE WAS DEAD!!"

Then this dynamic speaker eyes the audience and says, "Some of you have money. Some of you have lots of stuff. Some of you have many friends. You only have one problem. YOU'RE DEAD!!"

Do you worry that you are on the verge of spiritual rigor mortis?

Check your pulse with this week's study on the promised Holy Spirit in our lives.

MONDAY

FOCUS:
Lord, give me an appetite for Your Word, an awareness of Your Presence, an active life for You. In Jesus' name. Amen.

Question #1: What or who is the Holy Spirit?

Christians have long taught that God is a trinity, Three Persons in One, though the word "Trinity" is never used in the Scripture. The Three Persons are the Father, Son, and Holy Spirit.

Christians also have taught that the Trinity is a mystery beyond our ability to comprehend. Examples of "three in one," like the egg being yoke, white and shell, or H_2O coming in the form of water, ice and steam, may be helpful, but are wholly inadequate.

Just as your dog can't fathom the meaning of $E=MC^2$ (and most of us can't either!), mere humans can't get a grasp on the Trinity. But that should not keep us from trying to know God as best we can. What do these Scriptures teach you about the nature of the Holy Spirit?

What is the Holy Spirit called in Romans 8:9-10?
"You, however, are controlled not by the sinful nature but by the Spirit, if the Spirit of God lives in you. And if anyone does not have the Spirit of Christ, he does not belong to Christ. But if Christ is in you, your body is dead because of sin, yet your spirit is alive because of righteousness."

"Spirit of _____" and, "Spirit of _____."

What bold statement is made in 2 Corinthians 3:17?
"Now the Lord is the Spirit, and where the Spirit of the Lord is, there is freedom."

How does Paul's last verse in 2 Corinthians 13:14 relate to the Trinity?
"May the grace of the Lord Jesus Christ, and the love of God, and the fellowship of the Holy Spirit be with you all."

With what is the Holy Spirit paralleled in Luke 1:35?
"The angel answered, 'The Holy Spirit will come upon you, and

the power of the Most High will overshadow you. So the holy one to be born will be called the Son of God.'"

And also in Luke 24:49 and Acts 2:1-4?

"'I am going to send you what my Father has promised; but stay in the city until you have been clothed with power from on high.'"

"'When the day of Pentecost came, they were all together in one place. ²Suddenly a sound like the blowing of a violent wind came from heaven and filled the whole house where they were sitting. ³They saw what seemed to be tongues of fire that separated and came to rest on each of them. ⁴All of them were filled with the Holy Spirit and began to speak in other tongues as the Spirit enabled them."

What do you learn in comparing Matthew 12:28 with Luke 11:20?

"But if I drive out demons by the Spirit of God, then the kingdom of God has come upon you."

"But if I drive out demons by the finger of God, then the kingdom of God has come to you."

With what is the Spirit involved in Genesis 1:1-2 and Psalm104:30?

"'In the beginning God created the heavens and the earth. ²Now the earth was formless and empty, darkness was over the surface of the deep, and the Spirit of God was hovering over the waters."

"When you send your Spirit, they are created, and you renew the face of the earth."

Based on your study today, how would you describe the nature of the Holy Spirit?

 PRAYER:
Holy Spirit, help me to know you just as I know the Son and the Father.

TUESDAY

FOCUS:
Confess any held or hidden sin before trying to learn more about God.

Question #2: What does the Holy Spirit do?

Before studying the Scripture, answer the question based on your experience. What do you think the Holy Spirit has done in your life? List as many things as you can think of.

How active would you say the Holy Spirit has been in your life?

❏ Very ❏ Somewhat ❏ Little ❏ None

What does the Holy Spirit do in the believer's life according to . . . ?

Mark 13:11
"Whenever you are arrested and brought to trial, do not worry beforehand about what to say. Just say whatever is given you at the time, for it is not you speaking, but the Holy Spirit."

John 16:13
"But when he, the Spirit of truth, comes, he will guide you into all truth. He will not speak on his own; he will speak only what he hears, and he will tell you what is yet to come."

Acts 2:31
"Seeing what was ahead, he spoke of the resurrection of the Christ, that he was not abandoned to the grave, nor did his body see decay."

Acts 8:29 and 13:2

"The Spirit told Philip, 'Go to that chariot and stay near it.'"

"While they were worshiping the Lord and fasting, the Holy Spirit said, 'Set apart for me Barnabas and Saul for the work to which I have called them.'"

Romans 8:13

"For if you live according to the sinful nature, you will die; but if by the Spirit you put to death the misdeeds of the body, you will live."

Romans 8:16

"The Spirit himself testifies with our spirit that we are God's children."

Romans 8:26-27

"26 In the same way, the Spirit helps us in our weakness. We do not know what we ought to pray for, but the Spirit himself intercedes for us with groans that words cannot express. 27 And he who searches our hearts knows the mind of the Spirit, because the Spirit intercedes for the saints in accordance with God's will."

1 Corinthians 12:7-11

"7 Now to each one the manifestation of the Spirit is given for the common good. 8 To one there is given through the Spirit the message of wisdom, to another the message of knowledge by means of the same Spirit, 9 to another faith by the same Spirit, to another gifts of healing by that one Spirit, 10 to another miraculous powers, to another prophecy, to another distinguishing between spirits, to another speaking in different kinds of tongues, and to still another the interpretation of tongues. 11 All these are the work of one and the same Spirit, and he gives them to each one, just as he determines."

Galatians 5:22-23a

"But the fruit of the Spirit is love, joy, peace, patience, kindness, goodness, faithfulness, gentleness and self-control."

In which of these ways has the Spirit worked in you? (Circle) each way you have experienced his activity.

Are there any of the above ways that you really want him to work in you? Put boxes around them.

PRAYER:
Ask the Spirit to work in you in the ways you just boxed! Jesus said, "Ask and you shall receive."

WEDNESDAY

FOCUS:
Did God answer your prayer of yesterday? If so, thank him.
If not, consider why not.

Question #3: How can I receive this Holy Spirit?

Do I have the Holy Spirit at certain times, but not at other times? Can I have the Spirit if I am not experiencing very much of the fruit of the Spirit — love, joy and peace? What if I don't feel the Holy Spirit inside me?

God's promises are solid gold. If he says it, you can trust it. But promises also can have conditions. "If you ask nicely, you can have more cake." What must you do to have the assurance the Holy Spirit is with you?

Acts 2:38
"Peter replied, 'Repent and be baptized, every one of you, in the name of Jesus Christ for the forgiveness of your sins. And you will receive the gift of the Holy Spirit.'"

Luke 11:9-13
"⁹So I say to you: Ask and it will be given to you; seek and you will find; knock and the door will be opened to you. ¹⁰For everyone who asks receives; he who seeks finds; and to him who knocks, the door will be opened.
"¹¹Which of you fathers, if your son asks for a fish, will give him a snake instead? ¹²Or if he asks for an egg, will give him a scorpion? ¹³If you then, though you are evil, know how to give good gifts to your children, how much more will your Father in heaven give the Holy Spirit to those who ask him!'"

Circle the above steps you are sure you have taken.

Is the Holy Spirit earned or is he received as a gift, according the above verses?

Can one be a Christian and not have the Spirit? Read Romans 8:9.

"You, however, are controlled not by the sinful nature but by the Spirit, if the Spirit of God lives in you. And if anyone does not have the Spirit of Christ, he does not belong to Christ."

Yes _____ No _____

Chinese writer Watchman Nee tells us to stop praying, "Lord, fill me with your Spirit" and start saying, "Lord, thank You I have the Spirit!"

Some may say, "I have taken the steps indicated in these passages, but still don't feel the Spirit." Motive is also involved in God's gift of the Spirit. What does James 4:3 say?

"When you ask, you do not receive, because you ask with wrong motives, that you may spend what you get on your pleasures."

Do you want the Spirit so you can FEEL BETTER or FOLLOW BETTER?!

What else might hinder us from experiencing the Spirit? Read Ephesians 4:30-31.

"³⁰And do not grieve the Holy Spirit of God, with whom you were sealed for the day of redemption. ³¹Get rid of all bitterness, rage and anger, brawling and slander, along with every form of malice."

Oswald Chambers in *My Utmost for His Highest* states that if you really want to know and understand the Spirit, one minute of absolute obedience will teach you more than 100 hours of study. Have you ever surrendered yourself fully to the Spirit's rule in your life?

 PRAYER:
Holy Spirit, thank you for taking up residence in my life. I give You the keys to every door, the right to every decision, the rule in every deed. Amen.

THURSDAY

FOCUS:
Thank God that the Holy Spirit was present with you all day yesterday.

Question #4: How can I walk in the Spirit?

What ought to control the Christian's life? Read Romans 8:6-9.

"⁶The mind of sinful man is death, but the mind controlled by the Spirit is life and peace; ⁷the sinful mind is hostile to God. It does not submit to God's law, nor can it do so. ⁸Those controlled by the sinful nature cannot please God.

"⁹You, however, are controlled not by the sinful nature but by the Spirit, if the Spirit of God lives in you. And if anyone does not have the Spirit of Christ, he does not belong to Christ."

How is this control achieved? Read Galatians 3:1-3.

"¹You foolish Galatians! Who has bewitched you? Before your very eyes Jesus Christ was clearly portrayed as crucified. ²I would like to learn just one thing from you: Did you receive the Spirit by observing the law, or by believing what you heard? ³Are you so foolish? After beginning with the Spirit, are you now trying to attain your goal by human effort?"

       ❑ 1. intense effort

       ❑ 2. confident trust

Christians often complain, "I don't feel the Spirit." What does 2 Corinthians 5:7 say about that? ("We live by faith, not by sight.")

Which should you believe — feelings and emotions or God's Bible promises? Read 1 Corinthians 3:16. ("Don't you know that you yourselves are God's temple and that God's Spirit lives in you?")
